"ADJUSTING" TO A CAREER IN PROPERTY & CASUALTY CLAIMS

A Guide For Current (And Future)
Insurance Claim Adjusters:

A Positive Outlook On The Profession,
Combating The Stressors, Tips For Success
And Being Happy With Your Career Choice.

By Chris Casaleggio

ISBN: 9798648210615

To the professionals I have learned from over the years, including the managers and mentors who have spent their valuable time teaching me. Many others have also inspired me along the journey. Special thanks to Patrick Kelahan for his contributions/input.

I would also like to thank my parents. They find it humorous to refer to me as "The King of Claims" as it's similar to the title of one of their favorite shows, that long-running comedy based in one of the five boroughs of NYC. If this book is a success, then I will buy them the farm I promised to purchase them when I was younger. However, technical insurance books are not usually best-sellers, so I cannot confirm where that farm may be located. ☺

CONTENTS

*"**ADJUSTING**" to a Career in*

*Property & Casualty **CLAIMS***

INTRODUCTION

Where It All Began

As early back as I could remember, I wanted to be an insurance claims adjuster. My parents placed a sample homeowner's policy in my crib as a subtle test of my future aptitude, and I immediately gravitated toward it. Over the years, my obsession grew. Settling clear cut parked car accidents and eventually advancing into more complex coverage matters. By age 13, I was perusing large loss reports during recess. How I wished I could be part of a litigation roundtable someday to provide my thoughts on the direction and negotiations of a high severity damages case. While other classmates used their free time to participate in silly organized sports such as baseball and soccer, I began a fantasy claims pool. My friends and I would sort plaintiff medical records to determine who could evaluate the injuries closest to the settlement amount. Some may say in essence, that I was "born" to be a claims adjuster.

Falling Into Claims

If you believed my introductory paragraph, then you may need to have your head examined by a doctor. While you are at it, go ahead and set yourself a $15,000 initial injury reserve to start. Sorry, force of habit for a casualty claims adjuster.

Nope, not even close. Believe it or not, the truth is that I wanted to become a professional athlete when I was older. I was even thinking, why not be one in two major sports while I'm at it, might as well shoot for the stars. Like most of you reading this right now, you probably never dreamed of a career in the insurance claims world. I fell into the field like most adjusters out there. I started out of college as a journalist, and it was a lot of fun. However, there was intense competition coupled with low pay and few opportunities for advancement at the time. I wanted to afford nice things, move out on my own and travel the world on my vacation days. That is when an opportunity came along from a friend whose carrier was hiring several claim adjusters to start a new auto unit. All I needed was a degree, no experience, and my current salary would quickly double with the move. Intriguing, to say the least.

No Experience Necessary

Wait a minute. But what is a claims adjuster? What did I sign up for? Well, it didn't matter. They wanted to train me from A to Z. They liked my attitude and were willing to take a chance. The salary increase meant I could maybe even move out of my parents' house. What did I have to lose?

I applied, interviewed, and was hired within a few weeks. Only one slight issue, I had not quit my job as a full-time writer. I started work at the insurance carrier with a perfect 7:00 am – 3:30 pm schedule and decided since my other job involved mainly work after 4:00 pm, and many weekends I was going to try both. It took three months of both jobs (and many sleepless nights meeting writing deadlines) before I finally had to make the decision. I decided that I was going full steam ahead with adjusting claims. I have not looked back since and have been involved in insurance since that day.

My Writing Makes Its Return

Perhaps this book is an homage to my early writing days, but it is specifically based around the lessons learned over the years in the insurance claims industry. I have shadowed the best adjusters and have also spent time around some who were not so good. Sometimes many of the best lessons are when mistakes are made. How else does one learn? From the eager employees who rose straight to the top to the most cynical and burnt-out who warned me to leave before it was too late (oddly enough, they never left themselves). I have learned from great supervisors and also from those I could see were subpar and even manipulative. Lessons seemed to be at every corner and each of the companies that I spent time with adjusting claims.

All On The Same Team

There is a camaraderie in the industry and being part of a team environment. You are all in the same boat. You all are showered with an abundance of claims that at many times are just too much for any of you to properly handle. But you get through it and take some knowledge away from every file. And your teammates are there for advice or just to listen about everyday life topics. They are even a great source of laughter when you are able to eavesdrop on some of their entertaining phone calls with claimants.

Positives Overlooked; Industry Is Evolving

The insurance industry has a lot of great benefits, but in society, it seems that the adjuster is sometimes underappreciated. Some have gone so far as to reword the title of the claims adjuster position, so it sounds more important. Yes, it is a difficult and stressful job at times, but I am here to tell you about the great benefits you may (or may not) realize at face value. The times are changing with the incorporation of new technology into claims. InsurTech is attracting new entrepreneurial minds, and young talent is ready to enter the workforce with emerging skill sets that could take the field to new heights. I've seen countless examples of newer adjusters working hard to rise to manager roles with relative ease. High-level positions are available with many seasoned vets retiring, and this trickles down to great opportunities for the younger staff. Ultimately this also means more dollars in our pocket (and at a younger age) than in the past, which no one is complaining about.

Yes, we know about the stressors, but just like in any job, sometimes we fail to see the positives. Or, for that matter, we fail to see the negatives of other professions outside of insurance that we deem so "glamorous." I hope to provide the current (or future) adjuster with a new approach of thinking. Many are very happy with this career choice, and it can be just as lucrative and rewarding depending on your mindset (and blocking out the voices of those who may be jaded).

A Year Off In Claims

I've always thought that as Americans, we should take a chapter from our international brethren who often go on a "gap year" out of high school to refocus and confirm where their interests lie with regard to future studies. What if the gap year consisted of a full-time role in insurance claims? Can you imagine that? One might pay their dues, work hard, and take away many life lessons. Imagine how much you could learn and be ready for in the real world? Sure, you might dislike the position at the adjuster's desk, but you can't deny that it will make you more well-rounded on topics such as investigation techniques, customer service, negotiations, legal skills, construction methods, medical terminology, meeting deadlines, and most importantly that sense of urgency to complete tasks that adjusters perform so well.

Refocus And Realize What You Have

I hope you enjoy what I have put together and can take away a few tips to further your career. Perhaps it can help you take a step back and realize what you already have or help you refocus and find out where you really want to be. I have geared this towards the life of a property or casualty claims adjuster, but its points will translate to anyone in various areas of the claims industry. I hope the small investment is worth it to you in the long run.

Born To Adjust

And in full disclosure, I have used the "no one is born to adjust claims" speech many times. And truth be told, there was only one person who disagreed. He is a true unicorn of the industry and has a strong pedigree from a long line of insurance overachievers. He admitted to me that his first childhood book was indeed an insurance policy, and he is quite proud of it. If he was being honest, then I certainly must give him a shoutout and the solid, well-respected career he has built that will surely be passed along for years to come.

PART 1: PROPERTY & CASUALTY BASICS

A CAREER AS A P&C ADJUSTER

So, you want to become a property & casualty claims adjuster? Or perhaps you are a seasoned adjuster in need of a fresh perspective? Or maybe you are interested in getting into a new area or field of claims?

I am here to delve into a general overview of the process and offer advice to the adjuster looking to excel in this career path. With everything, there are pros and cons (which we will cover). Additionally, I will try to offer a new perspective or thinking rather than the initial negative reaction to some of these cons that can stress out many veteran adjusters.

Recently, I was discussing the shortage of adjusters in the industry with a former colleague at a large carrier. I learned that within 10 years the starting salary for the entry-level claims adjuster now has gone up by $20,000 since when I began. That's a big leap which tells the story of a workforce that is near retirement as the industry is hoping to attract an infusion of new talent.

Overall, the industry is lenient in its requirements as well. You need not study insurance-related coursework or Risk Management in college. A college degree of any course of study usually gets you in the door faster but sometimes one is not required at all. You can even work your way up from the bottom in this industry without having an undergraduate degree. A winning attitude and good customer service skills will take you a long way in securing a position at a carrier in the property & casualty field.

How Do You Obtain A Claims Position?

You can locate open claim adjuster positions by searching job posting websites such as Indeed, Glassdoor, Monster or LinkedIn. The job title or description may reveal the type of position offered, such as a property or casualty claims handler, or sometimes both.

Creating a basic resume and cover letter tailored to the opening and highlighting your experience would follow next. Be sure to incorporate how some of your past job experience or studies may have shown your ability to handle the role (such as customer service skills that may apply).

Using keywords similar to those in the posting may also help your chances of an interview as many companies run resumes through software to find the best candidates before forwarding for review. Next might be the phone screening from human resources or straight to an interview with management.

Preparing for the interview is important as usual in any process and time should be taken to research sample behavioral questions and scenarios online so you can be fully prepared. If you do not have specific experience that is suitable then it is always beneficial to have examples whether from school or more recent employment that thoroughly answer the questions as they are evaluating your critical thinking skills. Most carriers are willing to train the right person for the role regardless of their experience for entry-level claims.

Finally, a positive attitude trumps all and is refreshing so make sure to show a willingness to learn and improve. The industry loves adjusters who are eager. Often is the case that the manager you are interviewing with was once in your shoes when they started, bringing little experience but a winning attitude ready for a new challenge.

THE CLAIMS PROCESS

What Is A Property Claim?

To further breakdown property & casualty we start with a property or a "first party" insurance claim. This is because it is between the policyholder (first party) and the insurance carrier (second party). A simple example of this would be a homeowner filing a damages claim with the insurance company based on property that is covered under the insurance policy.

The insurance policy provides a promise to the insured and the adjuster is there to assist and fulfill that promise of loss investigation and if supported by the policy provisions, indemnity for claimed damage.

Another example might be while driving your vehicle you veer off the road and strike a fence causing damage to your car that you wish to claim and be reimbursed for the cost of repairs. If you own a home that is covered under an insurance policy you might make a claim for damage to your roof incurred during a recent windstorm. Your claim would be made with the insurance carrier and subject to your deductible. You would, therefore, receive a settlement based on the policy's conditions relative to how your carrier will pay a claim.

What Is A Casualty Claim?

A casualty claim is often referred to as a liability claim, which you will see used interchangeably in this book. This is when a claim is filed by someone else against your insurance policy. This is also called a third party claim.

Therefore, the duty of a liability adjuster is to protect the insured from an exposure they may have to another party. They may negotiate with a third party claimant to extinguish this exposure and settle the claim, preferably avoiding a drawn-out process that could involve litigation.

Merriam Webster defines a liability as "something for which one is liable." An insured may have committed an act that led to someone else's damages and may bear some responsibility. Or they even may have failed to commit an act they should have that led to a loss (a legal standard to determine negligence using a reasonable and prudent person as an example).

Consider the prior scenario mentioned where you struck a neighbor's fence with your car. The neighbor has extensive damage to their fence which they would like to have repaired. They report the loss directly to your insurance company as a casualty claim where an investigation of "liability" takes place to determine if they will be paid for damages as well as the appropriate amount.

Another example of a casualty claim might be when a guest visiting your home falls down the front steps that you performed a patchwork repair yourself on. This person suffers a broken leg and is out of work for months. They pursue a claim against the liability coverage of your homeowner's policy and an investigation is launched to determine whether they will be compensated for their damages based on possible negligence.

In this type of liability claim, the position may also be referred to as a "bodily injury" claims adjuster.

What Do Property & Casualty Adjusters Do?

(The Claims Process in a Nutshell)

Step 1: The Loss Occurs

-Reported to Carrier or Insured's Agent

-Received by Intake Unit

-First Report/Notice of Loss Generated

-Claim Number Created

-Scope of Claimed Damage is "Triaged"
(Method of inspection is determined)

-Assigned to an Adjuster
(*or a virtual inspection option may be offered)

A loss happens of some variety (whether a property loss for damage to the insured's home, or a liability loss such as a car accident in an intersection, or a pedestrian slips on ice on the sidewalk of a business). This begins the claim process.

A claim has been reported by the insured (or maybe the claimant depending on the type of loss). A liability claim can be reported by either party or through an attorney, placing the insurance company on notice that their insured may have been liable for a loss that took place (which the adjuster will need to investigate to determine if a duty was breached).

This notice can also arrive via phone call, email, fax or an agent notification of the loss. Notice has been given to the insurance carrier of a new loss and the investigation will follow in a timely manner. The claims intake team records the initial information that has been reported or called-in by one of the involved parties. It is the carrier's responsibility to acknowledge this report, assign a claim number and an appropriate level representative to handle the claim from the basic steps through resolution. At many carriers, a computer system might identify the severity of loss and assign it to a senior representative who generally handles the most complex losses which may involve extensive damages or injuries.

Step 2: Review New Claim and Policy

-New Claim on Adjuster's Desk
(*or to a virtual claim queue*)

-Review of Loss Details

-Check of Policy/Coverage Review

-Basic Information Confirmed

A new claim file lands on your virtual desktop as the adjuster. It is time to review the information received from intake as well as the policy. Details will be re-confirmed at the contact stage but here the adjuster will confirm the reported date of loss matches the policy and falls within the coverage period. Often a claim might be reported with incomplete phone numbers and the adjuster may need to contact the agent for up-to-date contact information of the policyholder. If this is a casualty or liability claim, then there is often an accident or police report to order.

In the virtual claims world (which is becoming more commonplace) the insured presents the facts of loss and proof of claimed damage via online or smart device application capture. There are digital claim services being developed that may allow claim handling to bypass an adjuster's full involvement, with artificial intelligence methods providing damage assessment and repair scope.

If able to do so at this point the adjuster may verify coverage. If not, further information may be needed, and if any issues exist the policyholder will be alerted of these depending upon the extent, e.g., over the phone, through a letter or more extensive analysis.

At this stage of the liability claim you may need the facts of loss as the third-party claimant may have reported the claim details which have yet to have been confirmed. The adjuster will review the known facts and get an idea of the direction their interview may go upon the upcoming first contact. In some instances, the initial statement taken when the claim was reported may provide a general idea of what took place, or it may provide little to no details making it still a mystery.

The claim system may auto-generate an index on the parties involved or the adjuster may need to do this on their own to see if there are other applicable prior losses for the involved parties. Initial claim acknowledgment letters may also be sent out at this stage depending on the state laws and requirements.

Step 3: Obtain All Statements

-Begin Investigation, Speak with All Parties

-New Info to Assess Additional Documents Needed

-Address Timeliness Standards, Mitigate Damages

-Begin Thinking about Reserves

Contact the insured for a statement right away. It is always best to try for one that is recorded as it will help down the line should the file go on for years or reach litigation (the same for the claimant and any witnesses). Leave voicemails and follow-up with letters if you are unable to secure contact. Make multiple attempts and try different times of day if needed to have a better chance.

After you have secured the insured's statement based on the claim you may be able to move forward and fully confirm that coverage exists. If this is a liability claim, you will also need to contact the claimant, along with any other parties involved (such as passengers in a vehicle or witnesses to the loss).

Make sure that you address timeliness standards as it pertains to the potential to mitigate damages. For instance, a non-drivable car might be incurring storage fees at a tow yard or emergency home repairs at an insured's building might be needed so that the damages do not worsen drastically. A reminder should be extended to the insured verbally during the statement process and followed up with a letter to confirm the conversation.

Given what has been obtained at this point, you will determine whether additional information and documents will be required, or perhaps you may have enough information already to consider posting a file reserve.

Step 4: Gather Documents, Investigate & Reserve

-Follow-up Items Needed

-Review the liability

-Post Reserves

Which documents will be needed for this case? Each scenario will be different. For the simple auto property damage case you just may only need the police report, the photos and estimates of the vehicles (usually obtained by an appraiser assigned from your company).

Are the facts consistent with what has been reported? Does the point of impact on the vehicles match from the appraiser's photos? If there are reported injuries how does the damage on the vehicles match up? If there is little to no damage on the vehicle and the claimant reports a major injury, then that will require further investigation.

There are often times a scene investigation may be warranted or a traffic light sequence in an auto claim (which can be performed by the adjuster online, in-person or through the use of a vendor). Often you must weigh the costs involved; for a very minor property damage case you are not likely to engage an expert such as an engineer that may cost $2,000 to help you investigate the loss. Instead, you will likely investigate and research the information yourself and negotiate directly with the claimant over the question of fact. With adjusting, you must be mindful of your expenses at all times and examine whether they are an investment in the outcome of the claim. A claimant always has the possibility to go through their own first party coverage, receive 100% of their damages and then have their company subrogate against the alleged at-fault party (or your insured). The downside for them though is that they likely have to pay their deductible upfront and it may take months to receive it back.

A first party property claim may need no further information besides a statement, estimate and photos of the damages at the time when a check can be sent to the insured (minus their deductible). Sometimes, it may not be so cut and dry how the loss took place. Insurance is supposed to be there stemming from a sudden or accidental loss. However, often may be the case that the loss has been ongoing for some time (even years) and that the problem was due to a maintenance issue that the insured let go without rectifying. This likely will present a coverage issue to confirm or even require an engineer's review if more complex before making a decision.

Given the information you have at this stage and the specific company requirements, you may need to post an appropriate reserve at this time. Different carriers employ different measures. Some may have advanced analytics and determine that all property damage claims be set at a specified number to start such as $2,500; others will give you more time to uncover information about the loss. Injury claims may come from experience given similar facts of loss and damages alleged in certain jurisdictions from claims you have had prior. Consultation with your teammates and managers on the proper reserve number may be needed. You'll always need to justify your amount with supporting facts.

Step 5: Determine/Explain Liability

(Casualty Claims)

-Assess Liability

-Support with the Facts

At this stage, for the third-party liability claim specifically, you have all the party statements, the police report and photos/estimates of the damage. You are ready to determine liability. Whether you assess a number such as 50/50 liability, a range 75-90% or 100% liability on the insured, you must back them up with supporting facts.

Consider all of the party statements, the police report and the points of impact in an auto liability investigation. You may need to update your previously set reserves if new information has changed your stance. At this stage you will explain your decision to both your insured and the claimant and set the expectation for the settlement of the claim and what happens next.

If you choose to deny the claimant's case then an appropriate, policy wording based denial letter must be issued to the claimant. In addition, a phone call explanation of why the claim is being denied may also be needed.

In a case with disputed facts, the claimant who is making the claim against your insured can always be reminded that to collect 100% of their damages they may pursue a claim with their own insurance carrier under their policy. At that point their carrier may pursue subrogation and the carriers will then make a determination with supporting arguments who is to blame for the loss. The claimant may not like this suggestion as under their own policy they may be subject to paying a deductible. However, that is why they have insurance; to settle the claim on their behalf and make them whole (or in a similar situation to how they were prior to the accident).

If the carriers can't agree on the liability percentages for their respective insureds then the claim could be sent (each with their arguments and supporting evidence) to a neutral arbitrator to decide liability which is binding.

Step 6: Negotiation/Settlement/Payment

-Settle Insured's Claim (*first party property*)

-Negotiate with Claimant (*third party liability*)

-Secure a Signed Release (*third party liability*)

-Issue a Timely Payment

In this stage for a first party property damage claim you will settle by issuing a payment to the insured and any additional named insureds or contractual additional insureds, e.g., a mortgagee (or otherwise formally deny the claim if that is the decision made).

In the negotiation and settlement stage for a third party liability claim, you will be explaining your decision for resolution to the claimant and to determine if they accept your offer. You may also have a range of settlement (such as 70-85% for example) and therefore present your facts and negotiate with the claimant based on your arguments. You may leave yourself this range to concede arguments made by the claimant as this is a give-and-take process and not always a clear-cut settlement percentage. Or they may present further information that makes you revisit your liability determination.

Once the offer is verbally agreed to by the claimant your company may require a release to be signed and notarized prior to sending payment (usually claims above $500 without injuries). You will explain that the payment will be final and end the claim (and their right to pursue further claims for property damage). This should be understood by the claimant that they essentially are giving up their rights in exchange for a settlement to compensate them for the loss. In the event there is a supplement needed on a property damage case during a vehicle repair then the appraiser will be sent back out to deem anything additional and if it should be covered under the loss. The same situation would apply during a first party property claim if more damages stemming from the loss were confirmed. In that scenario, additional payments could be issued if warranted.

Once you have received the claimant's signed release you may issue payment. In the event of an auto case where a claimant vehicle is undergoing repairs you may also need to cover a rental car (or loss of use replacement) for the estimated amount of repair days on the appraisal.

In more complex cases, lawsuits may be filed if a claim cannot be resolved. This would then entail sending the claim to counsel to begin the defense process.

Step 7: Pay Expenses, Close File

-Review File for Closure

-Pay All Expenses

-Close File

Once the claim is settled (and all expenses are paid out) you may close your file. Often there are vendors used for investigative fees (appraisal costs, investigator expenses or even engineering experts that may have been used by the claim handler). These are paid timely and the file can be closed.

On a third party claim, once the release is signed and the claimant is paid then you have extinguished the exposure and protected your insured from any further liability for the claim incident.

Again, <u>this is a very limited account of the claims process</u> to give new adjusters a basic understanding of what takes place from beginning to end. There are many great resources and trainings available which cover the preceding categories extensively. I would encourage you to review those if interested in more of the nuances and complexities that are involved.

How Are P&C Adjusters Judged?

Adjusters are typically judged (or rated) at different times of the year. Perhaps at the quarter, midyear or even yearly depending on the company. They typically randomly sample a handful of files.

Accordingly, you are judged by your company's best practices with regard to your work product. They may differ from company to company but they normally measure a majority of these categories.

Please consider that file reviews are initiated by the carrier to help ensure uniform claim practices are performed, regulatory requirements are being met, and basics of customer experience are upheld. File reviews help ensure common practices are being conducted.

File Documentation
Are you clear and concise with documenting your files? If it is not found in the claim file notes, then the old adage is that "it did not take place!" Document everything, but refrain from using any sort of language that may be construed as bias. Be clear, concise and objective. This is also of great importance in the event a teammate

needs to assist on your file.

Contact
Are you contacting all parties in your claim file? Your company may have a 24-hour or similar contact standard. A good investigation starts with contact and if you don't call the parties associated with your file then you can't expect to be judged very kindly at review time. These customer service skills are paramount in the industry.

Coverage & Investigation
Are you thoroughly investigating coverage, liability and accurately assessing damages on your files? Do you have an action plan for capturing this information in your files?

Evaluation & Reserving
Have you evaluated liability and damages while setting appropriate and timely reserves? Have you updated your reserves with the receipt of new information? Are you requesting authority where appropriate and within your levels as deemed by management?

Negotiation & Settlement
Are you negotiating and settling files within your authority? Are you re-evaluating upon receipt of new information? Are you making timely payments and obtaining appropriate releases on liability files? After settlement are you identifying potential subrogation opportunities?

Other categories that may appear include communication skills, diary/task management and for more senior-level adjusters, litigation management. Working with business partners, vendors and those within other departments such as SIU (Special Investigation Unit), agents, brokers and underwriting is also important.

Many carriers now have switched to having adjusters write their own review with comments on how they feel they performed with regard to each category. Then managers will comment as to if they agree or not and provide a rating. Usually you will meet with your manager on a weekly, or monthly, or as-needed basis, so you have an idea of how you are performing in these categories and there are no surprises. It is always wise to jot down claim numbers as specific examples throughout the year when you have performed well or received compliments. It makes your life easier later on when you are trying to remember what took place early in the first and second quarter and you are faced with a deadline to fill out your performance review.

In addition, many carriers have an auditing team that may randomly sample files throughout the year to identify trends and opportunities in the office for improvement. Though the process is completely "random," I believe that Murphy's Law plays a role here as the auditors are quite adept at finding the subpar files that slipped through our "investigative" cracks. Those always seem to provide a reminder to work all of the files in your inventory and maintain strong diary management.

PART 2: A GOOD INDUSTRY TO WORK

JOB SECURITY

An insurance claims career, while not glamorous by title, is steady and reliable. The population around us live their normal lives and losses are a continuing part of that cycle. The need for insurance coverage and adjusters is not going to change any time soon. We live in a litigious society where actions are often deemed to be someone else's fault. We all need insurance to cover us in various aspects of life. It is recession-proof to say the least.

In 2020, we all witnessed an unprecedented pandemic as COVID-19 changed the world. With millions of Americans losing their jobs the result was complete devastation to the country. However, one industry proved secure as insurance companies were quite prepared to assume full remote working capabilities without missing a beat. A number of insurance CEO's announced without hesitation that their workforce's safety would remain at the forefront and they were ready to assume work-from-home duties for their staff. This was all while many other professions were contemplating their plans of whether to keep all their workers, but also if they were technologically capable of shifting to remote working options.

Sometimes we have a tendency as adjusters to compare ourselves to those employed in other occupations, such as our friends and family. Those who carry fancy titles and higher wages may seem appealing at first glance but when push comes to shove in a time of catastrophe many of those positions may not be a secure as we think.

As adjusters we also may build a pessimistic view of those making claims against a policy and can be suspicious of their intentions. We may think we've seen the same situation over and over or can identify fraud based on our vast experience. But at the end of the day the increase in claims reported just provides greater job security, so why not look at it as a positive?

In this position, if you handle your claims reasonably well, have good customer service and continue to build on your experience and handling, there is going to be an adjuster job for you somewhere. To be honest, I have even seen struggling adjusters that have applied elsewhere and surprisingly have earned a higher-paying role. The next carrier does not know what your reviews or metrics were. They just know you have experience and interview well enough, so they will pay you a bit more to join them. They have an open role long overdue to fill, a bunch of claims to pile on your desk before you even start, and you are hired with a clean slate.

Sure, claims can be stressful but think about if you were at a company and had to make a sales goals each month. Perhaps you had to sell a half-rate product and were putting in time on the weekends or at nights making calls and it kept you up at night. Not knowing if you'd have a job in a month or two. How about at a place where everyone wanted to work, and every new graduate was trying to get in and push you out the door? A negative for the insurance world overall is that there are fewer new candidates seeking this position out of college (we are trying to change that) but for right now that's good for you with less competition.

Based on the work, there never seems to be enough adjusters in supply and many more are retiring in the years to come. Computers just can't do the job and handle customer service aspects. More high-level roles are available each day as veterans of the industry retire. It's time to take advantage!

FLEXIBLE WORKING ARRANGEMENTS

The Flex Schedule

The majority of insurance carriers or third party administrators allow employees to work a flex schedule. This can greatly assist with your work-life balance whether you have kids that get home from school early, evening classes to attend or even a second job.

7:00Am - 330Am

Many casualty adjusters are at a desk and may have access to certain set shifts. A former colleague of mine began his insurance career for one reason, this flexible schedule. He was looking for a position where he could have benefits, a steady salary but most importantly allow him to pursue his passion (training for martial arts). To this day he has been at the same carrier due to a flex schedule that begins at 7:00 am. Being a morning person this works out perfectly for him. He begins his day early and then takes a mid-day half-hour lunch and is out the door by 3:30 pm to begin his training regimen. When I used to work this schedule, I had some very jealous friends in other professions who would be fighting rush hour to get home before 6:00 pm whereas I'd already been home for almost 2-3 hours. Most carriers allow such schedules and some offer the early shift option for employees in good standing.

Other former colleagues followed this schedule to beat the traffic home and live in a more affordable area. Another bartended part-time in the evenings. Another good option in this career is to use the time to obtain a master's degree part-time in the evenings or further one's education. Most carriers after a year of employment may even contribute to tuition costs.

10:00Am – 6:00Pm

While the flex schedules can vary between core hours, some also have the option of sleeping in (for the night owls). With some adjusters electing an early schedule there is a need for coverage later in the evening. Based on whether you work for a carrier in a specific time zone of the US this could be even later. Maybe you are the type who likes to go out a few nights a week? This assists in getting those much-needed hours of sleep. I used this for some time to catch up on sleep as I participated in a late-night sports league.

Work From Home

One of the newer options (since the pandemic) is fully remote working. A property adjuster traveling during the day to sites is normally doing this, but now the casualty desk adjusters are more and more working from home a few days a week to sometimes completely remote. The nice perk here is not using your time on the road, gas, wear and tear on your car and even your vacation days when you are slightly under the weather. You can also setup your schedule for the most part and run errands during the day, take care of pets, etc. I would caution against multi-tasking to take care of young children at the same time because it will be very difficult to succeed with the workload if you do not have enough focus. But when you want a coffee break it's a bonus to have the freedom to run down the street or take small breaks. There may also be associated home office tax breaks to take advantage of.

Saving on commuting and not sitting in traffic is a tremendous bonus. Carriers believe they get more out of an adjuster during the time they would have just been in the car on the way to work. Just be cognizant of distractions at home and make sure your day actually ends. I have seen those who work around the clock which is not healthy. Be sure to set an endpoint to the day and stick to it.

The 4-Day Work Week

Gaining industry traction is some carriers trying out a 4-day, 10-hour workweek. Think about having to only work 4 days a week and get Friday, Saturday and Sunday off. That can be used for a second job, or for traveling, or whatever you can think of. Less commuting and sitting in traffic. Maybe even a day less of paying for child care.

With the flexible schedules offered there is now more competition for these roles as attorneys are even looking to become claim adjusters. An attorney typically works very late hours and a role as an adjuster might not be as lucrative but may provide more time at home with regular hours. Plus, one can still work with the legal system and utilize many of their skills.

EDUCATION, NETWORKING & COWORKERS

Training, Licenses & Designations

The claims industry is very supportive of its adjusters and their continuing education. Adjusters should take advantage of training offerings that allow them to sharpen their skills. I recall the support at a carrier that I received when I was interested in a negotiation training that I thought could benefit my career. They paid to fly me out to Chicago and it was a memorable trip with many tips that I walked away with. I also met other coworkers from different offices that offered a new perspective and stories about claim handling in other jurisdictions. Great connections and friendships were made in the process.

If you don't want to travel, there are usually many online courses available on an array of topics. Personally, I felt the in-person classes were the most beneficial due to the face-to-face interaction.

It is also true that carriers will pay for adjuster licensing. Obtaining these state certifications just make you more valuable as an adjuster (and more appealing to other carriers should you decide to move on). Credits must be taken, however, to keep these licenses current throughout the years (another networking opportunity in itself).

Insurance designations are more involved, and many consist of a track of courses over a few years to earn. AIC or CPCU designations are preferable now when hiring some higher-level positions (and soon may be mandatory). If your company is paying for the books and testing costs, then why not go at your own pace and earn the designation? Some companies even reward adjusters with a small bonus for obtaining them. Once you have a designation it requires no further follow-up and you have a few more letters at the end of your name on your business card. If time involved is a consideration, then just go slowly and study at your own pace. You are not required to complete an exam right away until you are ready and have signed up for a testing window.

If your company wants to invest in your education (and building up your resume) why not let them?

Events & Conferences

A big plus of the insurance adjuster career can be the networking aspect. Joining one of the top organizations and attending their conferences can be beneficial for learning but also a lot of fun. CLM, PLRB and Perrin Conferences are just a few of the larger ones out there. Normally, when working at a carrier they are free (or a small fee) to attend. They may be local or anywhere in the US - and everyone enjoys a free trip to places like Orlando, Las Vegas or San Francisco now and then. The classes and education are great, along with meeting new adjusters from different companies.

Connecting and learning about what others do and how their carrier is setup is also a great benefit. Exchanging business cards or LinkedIn profiles can keep you in touch and build your network should you ever pursue a new opportunity later on.

These events are sponsored for the most part by vendors or law firms who may take adjusters out to happy hours, dinner/drinks and have parties or events to attract potential business. Know your company rules ahead of time when accepting anything from a vendor. Additionally, be careful giving out your business card if you do not want to be contacted (spammed) by them in the future.

Online Networking

While you may not have the time to keep up a fully engaged LinkedIn profile it is always good to stay in touch with current and former colleagues. Adjusters move around the industry frequently. Some of the adjusters I started my claims career with are in management positions all over the country. You always will have the opportunity to catch up later or reach out if you have an interest in what life is like at their carrier. Plus, the bonus for current employees recommending candidates for an open position will be even greater motivation for them to help you aboard their carrier.

You will meet many adjusters at trainings (within your company or outside) and it is a good idea to network with them. You never know when you may want to reach out to them or see if they are also attending a future industry event.

LinkedIn also posts job openings and if you are looking for work elsewhere you can allow recruiters to reach out to you by clicking on that setting. Sometimes carriers will target adjusters online whom they are interested in and have recruiters reach out directly to you so always keep your profile updated.

Great Coworkers

Before interviewing with a carrier, you may conduct some research. Whether you check Glassdoor, Indeed, or other websites for reviews and employee feedback, you will notice similar positives and negatives. One of the common elements of even the most negative review recounts praise for the great coworkers met at the office.

Typically, an ex-employee who was fired has the most interest in writing a scathing review, so obviously they should be taken with a grain of salt. Perhaps employees who really loved the company could be inclined to leave a review, but you don't get a great sample size of all workers leaving reviews. With that being said even the orneriest of former workers still seem to give props to their former colleagues.

Maybe it's the camaraderie of being in a stressful position and generally not competing with each other in a cutthroat environment, but there are great people working in claims. Some of the most knowledgeable and hardest workers call adjusting a career. As we say, some liability representatives are like doctors or lawyers without the degrees (or pay for that matter). Some property adjusters are experts in their craft and may have built homes themselves in their free time. The thing that also sets these folks apart is that they are willing to help their fellow adjusters (new or old). When you have a question or want to run by a scenario on a loss it is your teammates who are the trainers. Often, your supervisor's time is occupied and you are sent over to a senior adjuster.

A good training plan starts with perhaps being sent away to learn in a classroom atmosphere. However, the big lessons are learned throughout the years from your teammates. And they also seem ready and willing to pitch in when you are on vacation or out sick. Or even when you need to reach an insured after normal working hours, they are on the task to help out. They know if they are in the same situation, you'd assist them.

The lunchtime crew of coworkers is there to talk about claim scenarios as well. Or they are there to grab a drink after work and vent about management or share a laugh. They are a sounding board for your complaints. And when one leaves the carrier, many stay in touch and keep tabs on life at the new carrier to see how green the grass is elsewhere. If you are an in-office adjuster you are spending 40+ hours a week with some of your coworkers, and that is a lot of time to get to know them. Good and bad times shared, sprinkled in with that one fellow adjuster who has the most entertaining calls with insureds or attorneys that you can overhear on the other side of the cube.

That "all in the same boat" mentality brings adjusters together. You make a lot of friends in this profession if you are friendly and have a good attitude. Interact, make new friends and share war stories. Learn about other departments in your office too and your knowledge will only grow with future opportunities. Typically, when you ask a colleague for advice you will find they have already gone through the same dilemma. And that in itself, been there done that, is refreshing to know that you're not alone in claims.

LATERAL MOVES & ADVANCEMENT

If you experience burnout (or even boredom) as an adjuster, the good news is that likely sitting a few yards away is a whole other line of business. Many adjusters move around departments to gain a more varied skill set. It is typically encouraged by the company (better to move within than to lose a good worker to another). Most carriers encourage their employees to become well-rounded.

Perhaps you are handling workers' compensation claims and think that you need something different. Well, you can go a new route, maybe then you want to try property or even liability claims. Where do your interests lie? Check your company job openings to see what is available. How about underwriting or a special role as a business analyst? What about a trainer and use your degree in teaching? There are many possibilities that you can talk with your manager about and make contacts or shadow someone to build toward.

Perhaps someday you want to be a risk manager for a company that is not an insurance carrier, well gaining workers' compensation, auto and liability or property experience would give you the skills you may need to do that. Relocating will give you even more opportunities if you are able to do it. When there's a need in another location you may have a chance to go into a higher position than if you stayed in your current office.

Another department could have a need for adjusters and there might be a quicker path to a management role. Maybe you have an interest in a certain niche of the business. If there are responsibilities that may be more in line with your skills, why not try it out? Normally these lateral moves require that you are in good standing at the company and the hiring manager from the other department will likely have access to your yearly review.

Consider a liability auto adjuster wanting a change of scenery. Research the following positions and how the duties may align with your interests:

Examples of "claim handling" positions
Property Adjuster (CAT Team)
General Liability
Subrogation
Workers Compensation
PIP (Medical)
SIU (Fraud)
Inland Marine
Environmental
Vehicle Damage Appraiser

Examples of "non-claim handling" positions
Underwriting
Sales
Human Resources & Recruiting
Analytics/Predictive Modeling
Operations
Training/Learning & Development
Marketing/Communications

These are just a few of the different areas you could transfer into depending on the business your carrier writes. Another consideration is if you want to handle personal or commercial lines claims. It is good to have experience in both and any change will just give your resume a boost and show your dedication to the company.

LEARNING, INVESTIGATION & HELPING PEOPLE

Great First Job

Whether you want to make it a career or just a first job out of college there is no denying the skills you will obtain in a claim adjusting position pertain to a number of other fields.

Depending on the line of business, you may learn investigation techniques, accounting, medical or legal procedures and terminology, customer service skills, negotiation skills and the ability to meet deadlines. You will practice business writing skills and compiling reports and letters. The list goes on of the many skills you can take from your time as a claims adjuster.

The benefits are also solid for someone in need of medical, dental, vision and a 401K. The paid time off, holidays and flexible work schedules also make it an appealing choice.

Whether you stay in the industry or move on after your first claims job, it will teach you a number of important life skills.

Helping People

Claim adjusters are there for some of the worst aspects of people's lives (in which they try to bring about a resolution). Natural disasters, fires, catastrophic events or auto accidents with injuries to name a few. However, we have the opportunity to be on the front line and help those in need. That's a pretty good feeling.

We can meet insureds and help them get back on their feet. We can listen to their needs and give them a chance to tell us everything they want to get off their chest. Many customers won't speak to the claimant carrier and insist they want to talk to their own company first before they do anything. We have their back. We are the listeners. They pay a premium in the event they ever need us. So, the one time perhaps they do it's important we are there for them.

Not many people are familiar with the process of a sheriff knocking on their door and handing them a summons and complaint. Imagine the feeling of an elderly person receiving a notice that they are being sued for a small fender bender which they forgot had even happened years prior. We have the ability to calm those fears and explain that while they may have forgot, we have been working to investigate the case for them all along and will be providing them a full defense.

We even are helping third parties whom our insured has wronged. We can ease the pain and anger by compensating them and showing that we care about their well-being and inconvenience. We can make things better and ease tension. Sometimes even an apology to a third party claimant will go a long way to settling a case because often that is something they wanted from the start.

Helping people in times of catastrophe is a great feeling. Don't forget how much of an impact you have on the healing process of the people you speak with on a daily basis.

Something New Each Day

They say that the attention span of the average human is

dwindling each day. Well that's fine in the adjusting world because you have a new claim each day (and usually multiple times a day) to keep your attention. Each claim may present an interesting investigation ready to be undertaken. Many other careers see the same thing over and over but in the general liability arena you could see the following five claims assigned to you in a week:

1. The insured was walking his dog when his Jack Russell terrier bit his neighbor who needed 10 stitches and is now pursuing a pain and suffering claim.

2. A claimant's apartment and belongings suffered fire damage after purchasing a telescope from the insured who failed to warn that this scenario was a possibility.

3. The insured vehicle lost control on an icy road and veered onto residential property striking a home and causing damage to a garden of rare flowers.

4. A fight broke out at a restaurant after a condominium board meeting in which the claimant alleges a traumatic brain injury.

5. An audience member re-aggravates a pre-existing neck injury when a member of the band at a concert decides to go on an impromptu crowd surf.

The examples are endless. But these five claims could be on your desk at any given time. Chances are you may need to further research these cases. Perhaps it's a good time to bring in an expert to assist (such as in scenario 2 a fire investigator or in scenario 3 a rare florist for a quote). Regardless, these can add some flavor to your day.

BENEFITS & PERKS

Health Insurance

Most companies offer health benefits such as medical, dental and vision plans. Life insurance and options for health savings accounts with competitive 401K packages are mostly standard. You'd be surprised how many companies elsewhere do not offer workers a 401K (some that even pay their employees very high yearly salaries) but this is mostly standard in the insurance careers industry so it is an excellent place to start.

Tuition Assistance

Another great benefit of working in claims is that most carriers will help assist you with tuition if you decide to go back to school. Many clerical claims positions do not require a degree, so it is possible to work your way up the ranks without one and then go back to earn your bachelor's degree.

Many adjusters may choose to work towards a master's degree as well in their free time. You might even be able to set yourself up with a flexible schedule (early claims shift) during the day that allows you to go to class in the evenings. It's a great benefit and shows that the insurance industry likes to invest in their employees.

The amount of assistance available may depend on the degree. However, if your plan is to someday work in another industry, this may also be a way to use your time wisely while working as an adjuster.

Time Off

Whether you want to refer to them as PTO (paid time off), vacation or sick days they can be quite good when compared to other professions. It is also something that you can usually negotiate if you have experience when joining a new company.

If you are an adjuster who also has the ability to work from home time to time this is even better. If you are not feeling well or have an appointment your manager may let you work from home so you do not need to burn a PTO day. That can really help you save days to use exclusively for vacation.

Another plus is that you can go away for 1-2 week vacations where you have a team that can assist on your files in your absence. Sure, they may not do a better job than you would but at least there is coverage. In some professions there is no backup for the work (it is their responsibility and no one else trained to do so and their customers are just put on hold). This leads to an unhappy vacationer checking their work emails and logging onto the computer while they're supposed to be enjoying a trip. Some professions also do not allow such lengthy trips away from the office but in my experience, I have seen a coworker (in good - standing with their files and management) get approved for a full month out of the office for an extended trip. Aside from being a teacher with the summers off, I don't know how many professions would even consider such a request.

When you are going to be out of the office on PTO, however, it is best to plan ahead. Tell your contacts and customers you think will likely call (the ones who demand constant contact) that you are out of the office that week and when specifically you will be back. Otherwise they will panic and reach out to your supervisor right away. Also placing a detailed out of office message is very important (with your away and return date as well as the backup contact). I always like to indicate to only contact my teammate if it is urgent and cannot wait (so that they do not get bombarded with calls).

The worst scenario is when an important business partner (high-net-worth broker as an example) calls while you are out and receives a general voicemail such as "I am out of the office." Their inquiry becomes instantly urgent and they assume that the adjuster may have been let go or went out on leave (or similar panic) and then call the manager.

It is a good idea to work ahead so you don't have any time bombs go off (you can't guarantee this, but you sort of have an idea which files may be an issue while you are away). Give your backup or supervisor a quick heads up of a few files that they may hear from someone on while you are out. Or if they should touch base quickly with a customer that you owe a call to. They will appreciate the notice. Never surprising your supervisor is always good advice to live by.

Other Perks

There are many other perks and discounts available to claims adjusters. Perhaps your company has an exercise facility in the building and can save you on a gym membership. Some carriers have dry cleaning services or a nurse onsite.

Phone discounts are usually available which save a good portion off your wireless bill. Some carriers pay for work phones. Sales agents, appraisers or some adjusters may be able to use a company car.

Pet insurance or other types of perks may be available, you just have to look for them on the company intranet page or ask your human resources representative.

PART 3: DEALING WITH POTENTIAL STRESSORS

TOO MANY CLAIMS

We were coming to this section eventually, so now that we are here, let's take an honest look at the stressors you will likely encounter in a claims role. Adjusting claims is not all sunshine and rainbows and that's obvious; but there are also ways of looking on the bright side and solutions to most problems we face in life.

Let's look at some of these and how to defeat negative thought patterns.

"I'm completely caught up!"

The above phrase has been rarely uttered by a claims adjuster. Anywhere.

"I'm drowning in a sea of claims!"

A common plea.

Well, this is a difficult one. That usually means you are a good adjuster and your manager may count on you to shoulder the load and hopefully by the end of the year you are rewarded with a bonus or merit increase. So, you can take that as a compliment and job security (which I mentioned previously as a positive).

Two adjusters I worked with had a different idea about it. They set good examples that I'll always remember. The first was worried when he didn't get a new claim for the day. When he received lots of work, he knew things were going well at the company. Another former colleague wanted to move up the ranks quickly and in time of trouble for the managers when they were in a bind with adjusters resigning, he did the unthinkable. He stepped up and asked for more work! He told his manager that he wanted all of the former employee's claims to handle (all 125 of them). Consequently, he moved up and six months later was a manager. Those efforts do not go unnoticed. Many adjusters may wonder why he would ask for more work? Well, simple, he wanted to make his manager happy, show his worth ethic and at the end of the day his career skyrocketed.

Some carriers just have too many claims (such as a pending of 200-250+). However, the caveat might be that their company is run that way and the reputation or product just may not be up to par with other carriers. They don't expect the level of detail or same level of handling elsewhere.

One startup carrier brought a former colleague in and overloaded him with transfer files right away. When he showed that he could handle it he was promoted to a team lead/manager position in less than a year (even though he was less experienced than many others).

This will always be the difficulty of claims but at the end of the day it is what you have signed up for. Keep yourself organized and avoid those unproductive days because you never know when the onslaught of new files will be coming. My record as an auto claims adjuster was 10 new claims on a Monday morning. Slow and steady, I made it through them. You can only do so much. Get the quick contacts and calls out of the way first and the most important items so that you can buy a little time to initiate the rest of the investigation. Don't let them sit, attack them head-on. These days will pass, and you will make it through. The company needs your help and it is always nice to feel like an important cog.

MONDAY MORNING FEELING

I Don't Want To Work Today!

As an adjuster we have all had this thought (and it usually comes on a Monday). I would look at my list of diaries and they looked overwhelming, plus the emails that came in over the weekend from an overzealous customer. My thinking was clear. I don't feel like doing much of anything this morning. However, if I don't do something productive, I am going to get buried with work later on.

If the urge not to work on that dreaded Monday morning came about, I would keep busy performing easier tasks or diaries for the next day to get them out of the way. If I had a strict deadline that day it was a different story though as I had to get it done. But I looked for ways to be productive on other tasks that I would soon be doing anyway to get them completed. If my Monday tasks looked unappealing, then let me clear out all of my Tuesday tasks, or Wednesday, or something that made sure I wasn't just wasting hours.

While it can be difficult as coworkers may ask you about your weekend, try to limit discussions/calls from your colleagues who have the "Monday Blues" and just want to chat. A quick 5-10 minute call is acceptable, but often there is that colleague looking for an excuse to stop by your desk for 30 minutes or more to gossip.

Taking breaks is much needed, but don't fall into the trap of being unproductive for long periods of time. It's just going to eat up your free time later in the day when a new claim rolls in or something important comes up out of the blue. Monday mornings happen to us all but be a little bit productive and you won't get too far behind.

DIFFICULT PERSONALITIES & COMPLAINTS

Angry insureds and claimants are in that mood for a reason so it's best to understand that right away. It's usually not with you personally. They probably have already provided a statement once and are now told you received none of that info from intake and they need to do it again. Or sometimes they've spoken to a medical adjuster and this is the third statement they've given (not so efficient they're thinking).

They've been inconvenienced, they've been wronged and maybe even missed a day of work or paid out of pocket for a rental car with no guarantee they will get their money back. This was the worst time of year to be in an accident and money is extremely tight. Now they are speaking to someone on the phone who they feel does not care about them personally and is just going through the motions taking a statement to move this process along. Or perhaps they're in pain from a loss and would appreciate a little more understanding. Maybe your insured was rude to them at the scene and their anger has been redirected towards XYZ Insurance for insuring such a bad driver.

Listen and understand these customers. Put yourself in their shoes. This may be one of their worst days in years (or their life) so a little uneasiness is normal. They want to be heard and to have some type of reassurance they will be assisted with their loss. When an adjuster responds to them in an unpleasant tone it will only escalate the situation. Treat their time as if it were just as valuable as your own. If you fail to do that the result will be them somehow reaching your manager with a complaint call. And some customers have the uncanny ability of getting a complaint or call to the higher-ups or CEO. A good tip again goes back to proper file documentation. When a claimant does call your manager, make sure your prior conversation with them is in the file notes explaining exactly what you told them. If they aren't, it's going to be open season for them to complain to your manager about the so-called promises you made to them when you last spoke.

Attorneys or public adjusters may sound upset for a different reason, as their negotiating ploy. The squeaky wheel gets the grease and intimidation against newer adjusters may go a long way. The funny part of the situation is that if their client had a stronger case then they probably could be more civil in their communications. However, it is just their style and when someone is negative and continues to pester you then your instinct is to want them to go away. You may pay them what they want and they win. Instead, challenge them with the facts. Know your file better than they know their client. Don't avoid the conflict calls and let the attorney know their behavior is unprofessional and you are here to discuss the merits of the case only. Let them file suit if they want to throw that in your face, you'll be ready.

A former colleague once responded to an attorney who threatened him with a lawsuit by saying, "Sure, you can file suit, we need to give more work to our panel attorneys anyway. They just took us out to this great football game last week and we sat on the 50-yard line. We need to give them some more business and their rates are reasonable, so we don't mind spending expense dollars on their firm." This was a creative (but highly unethical way) to take the wind out of a temperamental plaintiff attorney's sails. Better left for a laugh than to implement into one of your future calls, however.

"Let me speak to your supervisor."

Sure, they all want to see if they can obtain a better resolution from the supervisor. I would respond by saying that they are more than welcome to contact a supervisor who is going to convey the same exact message that I have. After they speak with him or her, we can pick up the conversation once again and look to move forward. When these parties talk to a supervisor it is ironic that they seem to change their tone and try to make it seem as if the adjuster was the one who created the problem. Fully documenting your file notes will be a great reference for your supervisor and discussion points you have previously put into this call.

Some parties may even go a step further to gain leverage by submitting a complaint to the department of insurance. Again, as long as you document your file and it is clear this is not one you mismanaged you should have little to worry about. Advise your supervisor immediately. They say that if you don't get one complaint in your time as an adjuster then you are not doing your job. On the contrary, if you start receiving letters of praise from claimants for your handling of their liability files, then you might be paying too much!

GOOD ADJUSTERS
PERFORM MOST
OF THE WORK

A colleague once told me about the 80/20 rule of claims. The Pareto Principle states that for many events, 80% of the effects come from 20% of the causes. When I complained that a few of us adjusters were getting so many important files he said that 80% of the work was being performed by 20% of the most reliable adjusters. While those numbers may have been over-inflated, most of the important files were indeed being handled (and trusted) in the hands of a smaller number of adjusters. These are the ones who know what to do with little assistance from management. They are more apt to have the important files sent in their direction because the supervisors know they will be handled well.

At first glance it seems unfair to be doing more work than your counterparts. However, resist the urge and time associated with complaining. You don't know your coworkers' situations. Be proud of the fact that you are a trusted employee. You are appreciated and should be rewarded at review time. If you do feel that you are behind with your work and need a break, speak with your supervisor. They will be more apt to give you the flexibility needed as you have been a key member of the team for years.

Keep note of the extra work that you perform for a later date when you fill out a yearly review. These adjusters given extra work and providing few headaches in return are the ones who will benefit when raises or promotions are on the horizon.

I remember times in a team setting where a manager asked us who wanted to assist with some transfer files. I knew in my head that no one would volunteer to do the extra work and at the end of the day it would come down to my manager telling me or another adjuster that we had to do it. Seeing that end scenario in advance I would usually volunteer for the work right away. Often my supervisor would give me the work I asked for with appreciation but sometimes I'd volunteer and because I did so often, he'd ask for another team member to step up and assist.

Don't worry about the claim inventory of other adjusters. It is difficult to compare given all the factors. Perhaps their work is more complex or deals with specific coverage knowledge. You don't know the whole story or their issues with their performance. It will waste your time investigating and management knows the associated circumstance.

If you feel there is a genuine issue and a lopsided amount of work, then by all means speak with your supervisor as it may make you feel better.

OVERLOADED WITH DIARIES

Do not set yourself up to fail!

Schedule your diaries and tasks efficiently and keep on top of them.

Do not overload yourself, especially on days when you have meetings, etc.

Keeping light on a Monday (or when the new claims are the highest) is a good idea. There are even adjusters who touch their files too often. Work them on one day to the fullest and then schedule them out at the next appropriate date. Some complex files may not have a need for an update for 60-90 days. Determine the best course of action based on each file.

Be smart, organize yourself and your emails. Don't fall behind on tasks that should be scheduled appropriately with minimal time committed.

LACK OF PRAISE & RIPE FOR CRITICISM

Claims move fast, and you may feel like in the eyes of management that you are only as good as the last one you handled. Bad verdicts can follow you around for years, and even the best handled claim can be viewed by someone in a negative way. You may have negotiated the heck out of a claim with a really excellent result, but another perspective could be that you over-reserved that same case. First party property adjusters are on the front lines meeting customers and delivering checks. They seem to be more apt to receive well wishes from the insureds.

On other lines of business (such as in liability) you may need to have a thick skin and realize that if you are still getting counted on by your supervisor and assigned difficult claims then you are doing a good job. It is often easy to lose sight of that fact.

Claim audits can be discouraging when you are told there are only four possible scores. It is then followed by "don't expect to get a 4 rating because that is like walking on water, it is extremely rare."

1 = unacceptable
2 = requires improvement
3 = satisfactory (meets most requirements)
4 = excellent

The metrics can be hard to meet. It is vital to work each file to the best of your abilities and let the chips fall where they may. The way I look at it you should not get overly upset because that is a claim auditor's job to find fault and ways to improve. If they did not, then there would be no use for a claims auditor. In essence they are protecting their own job by redlining your file with comments. I have been at companies where my files have been nitpicked and at carriers where I have been surprised they didn't fault me when they should have. Use these as opportunities where you can pick up a few tips to focus on moving forward with your claim handling. Advise your supervisor before they tell you about them on their own and you will win points. "I noticed a trend in my files reviewed and I will note that in this year's review so I can get better. If you have any advice or know someone on the team that does this well maybe I can sit with them and learn more."

It can be hard to understand, but you won't get an abundance of recognition for a job well done. Your reward will be more claims (perhaps more complex) coupled with trust from your manager. More work that they trust you to take care of and that won't make themselves look bad to upper management for giving it to you.

However, keep note of certain files that you have done a great job with somewhere on your desktop. A great settlement and negotiation, or an accurate medical evaluation or perhaps praise from a customer for your service are all good to keep handy.

The bottom line is that we do a difficult job and we may not receive praise. It may sometimes only be recognized with receiving more work (and trust).

CYNICAL ATTITUDE

The casualty adjuster may develop the attitude that claimants are motivated by self-interest. When you receive numerous claims per day you can become numb to the situation. Especially on the auto liability side when you have merely cosmetic damage to the vehicles involved and the claimant immediately elects to have major back surgery. The property adjuster may think some homeowners try to claim as much damage as possible (whether it relates to the loss or has been ongoing for years).

You may begin to distrust claimants and believe that they are looking only for the quick money grab. That they are of the belief that because your insured hit them, they are automatically now holding the winning Powerball ticket! Or that this fender bender has provided them the opportunity to go on permanent disability. Your insured was simply in the wrong place at the wrong time (the accident would have happened regardless because the claimant was looking for one)!

Wow, that is crazy talk. Take a step back now and recount what you just said. You can't take the claims process personally. Handle each based on the facts and perform your due diligence to investigate. Use your SIU/fraud team if something does not seem right. Check the internet and social media as you work to uncover the facts.

It can be difficult when you see an injured party receive a massive settlement amount and you have your doubts about if the accident really caused their injuries. That is not your problem though. Again, this comes back to job security. These claims are keeping carriers in business as insureds need to be protected with larger policies. And you have the chance on a complex claim to prove how good you are at your job. Upper management may have an eye on this incident so it's another opportunity to do a great job and move up the ladder.

Attorneys and public adjusters contribute to this cynical attitude that we develop. However, they are an advocate for their client. Most of the time, the "huff and puff" that they throw at you on the phone is just a technique that you can easily defeat by reiterating the facts of the case.

Don't take offense or get caught up in the things you hear and see every day. Brush them aside and thank them for their outrageous behavior which will keep you employed for many years to come.

SALARY CONCERNS

The first piece of advice is never to share your salary with your coworkers. No good can come from it. Either you will think you make too little and be upset, or someone else may have that feeling about you. You can research many websites online now and get an idea of what you can make with your experience. Keep it to yourself.

I remember the time I was taken aback by a fellow adjuster who asked me flat out how much I made. Even though he had 5-7 years less experience he believed we handled similarly complex claims (not true) and wanted my information. It was approached casually but I knew that the info would be passed around to others or to help build his case for a raise with a manager. I simply said that I would never share that information with anyone and that he could do the appropriate research or speak to his boss about it.

Some job postings now have the salary range, so you can check out Indeed or Glassdoor. Some salary ranges (based on geography of offices) are even shared by the company with adjusters.

One thing to keep in mind (and not get bent out of shape over) is that an adjuster who is 50 years old with 25+ years' experience that handles a similar assortment of claims as a 30-year-old adjuster with 5 years' experience is likely going to make more. That's just how it goes with a small merit increase every year. Don't get hung up on this because it can make you very upset over something you can't control.

If salary is an issue, have the appropriate conversation with your boss at review time. Make sure though that you have research to back up your numbers (your own personal investigation).

On the other side of the coin is that some people may prefer a better situation over more money. Perhaps an easier commute, a work from home schedule or other perks. Sometimes adjusters may not want more responsibility and prefer the situation they are in instead of spinning the wheel for a few more dollars in another role at a different company that is ultimately an unknown.

TOO MANY MEETINGS

Our time is valuable as adjusters and there seems to be little of it in our day. Ever look at the clock and see that it is already 4:00 pm with a million things left to do? What about those days where you have a long meeting or training that eats up a portion of your day?

If it's a last-minute meeting there is little you can do. But typically meetings are announced at least a week in advance, so it is imperative to plan ahead and organize.

If you have really important work to attend to and it may be in your best interest (and your manager's) that you skip a meeting, let your boss know. Perhaps you can sit in for some of the meeting and then step out to complete an important task that can't be rescheduled.

Otherwise, meetings are a good opportunity to share ideas and ask important questions. Sometimes they are attended by your supervisor's boss so it's a good opportunity to be ready. Staying silent in a team meeting is worse than being a participant and asking even the most basic question. Be involved and it will help advance your career. Unfortunately, the only defense to being pulled into too many meetings is to prepare appropriately ahead. Also, keep in mind that if you plan to move into a manager role in the future you will likely be a part of countless meetings.

COMPARING TO OTHER JOBS

So, you are a claims adjuster and maybe some people outside of the industry do not understand much about the role. Often is the case where an outsider asks, "Is that what you studied or went to school for?" And the answer is in most situations, no. When we were kids and dreaming about the future, few of us said we'd like to handle claims for a living.

Sometimes we get caught up in comparing our job to others. Especially when meeting a spouse's friends or coworkers we may need to explain what we do. We may compare ourselves to others with careers that seem more interesting. It is important to remember that while other jobs may make more money, there is always a trade-off. They may have to work a lot more hours, they may need to have more schooling (student loans), require more time away from family, can't work from home and involve a lot of pressure and stress.

We always think others have it better but most of the time that's not entirely accurate. We believe they may, but we don't always know the whole story. Perhaps they perform reasonably well but are up late at night wondering how they will make their sales for the month? Perhaps their coworkers cannot work together and are so competitive they are in fear of being pushed out the door. You don't deal with this much in claims. You are all needed as part of the team. Focus on your work and you will succeed. You are not expected to do everything yourself and be solely responsible for the business.

That friend who is making the huge salary in a job that seems too good to be true? Well maybe he doesn't have the same benefits, or lacks a 401K plan? Maybe it's even a contract job? Small companies can get bought out and are less secure. Situations change quickly. Don't forget as humans there are many of us who do not always tell the truth about what they really do for a living (shocking I know)! One of my non-insurance friends tells people that he owns property around the US that he rents out as a business and people are easily impressed as his lie is extremely detailed. However, I know the truth about his fabrication which is far from reality.

As adjusters we get the basic holidays off. Some jobs do not allow that and work weekends. Think about the most stressful jobs in the US. Police officers, firefighters, surgeons and others have the lives and safety of others in their hands.

While not a sexy career choice, claims is secure and offers many benefits that others may not see at first glance, but you can at least feel better about them.

EXPLAINING
WHAT YOU DO

I have found myself in many situations meeting strangers at an event and being asked what I do for a living.

"I'm an insurance claims adjuster."

This statement has been met with a variety of responses including the most negative that hits home.

"I had a claim recently. Insurance companies don't like to pay people, right?

You may also get a blind stare and reply such as...

"I see, what does that entail?"

Then I find myself trying to explain in a way that the typical person would understand and at the end of my description I have confused everyone even more.

Sometimes the words "claim adjuster" can have negative connotations to the outside world.

"Adjuster" could be defined as an insurance agent who investigates personal or property damage and creates estimates for settlements.

Well, is that all that we do? Does that sound very interesting to those outside of the industry? Some carriers have gone a step further and changed the title to "Resolution Specialist."

I had a friend who would vaguely tell people that he merely "handles investigations." That would spark interest and is for the most part true. You are not a private eye, but you do investigate and see something new every day. At the source you investigate coverage, liability and damages in casualty claims. A property adjuster is helping people on the front line and perhaps more customer service oriented. A liability adjuster may also have a vast medical or legal knowledge which doesn't translate when you only reply that you "handle claims" for a living.

The best way to explain it is with a real-life example. Think of an interesting claim scenario you had this year and the steps you took to resolve it. Don't sell yourself short and just say "I handle claims" because you do so much more. Give them a visual example of an exciting claim. Have a canned response ready to share the next time you are asked. Let's be advocates for the industry and educate.

Oddly enough, many people are most impressed by the flexible work arrangements that we receive in the profession. When I told outsiders that I work from home, or set my own schedule, that seemed to get the most intrigued response from my audience.

PART 4: WAYS TO SUCCEED AS AN ADJUSTER

ASSOCIATE WITH THE BEST

It has been said that you are the average of the five people you spend the most time with. Is that true at work as well? Think about that for a minute. Do you surround yourself with positive people and the leaders of the office?

Associate yourself with the adjusters you look up to. Everyone knows the reputation of the complainers. These adjusters may have been there 20+ years and have seen the times change, people come and go and always think the company is going in the wrong direction. However, they have pretty much made their bed and will continue along the same path. That is the only place they are comfortable until they retire.

Don't let others bring you down. Their experiences are different and do not pertain to you. Typically, while complaining they are leaving out key details of the story or something that they did which put themselves in the position in which they currently sit.

Refrain from office gossip. Good people will rise to the top. The disgruntled ones fill a role as well. They make you look better in comparison.

DOCUMENTING FILE NOTES

Always be sure to document your file notes properly. Every phone call or communication should be memorialized. If it is not in the notes, it did not take place. Your file notes can save you in times of need, such as when a customer claims they were never told of a critical fact or when they say that you never called them back.

When a supervisor gets a call, the first thing they do is put the caller on hold and check the file notes. If there is nothing documented, then the customer might be onto something. There is no defense to their claim that you completely botched their file or let it slip through the cracks. Then it is a customer service backtrack trying to satisfy the insured and save face with apologies and a better effort moving forward.

When you are out on vacation, it is also imperative to have updated notes so one of your team members can see what is going on in the file. This is another opportunity to impress your managers and teammates to show you are on top of your cases.

DEALING WITH
THE BOSS

The general rule is that supervisors do not like surprises. I think that is some of the best advice I have received for dealing with a boss. If something bad is coming on the horizon, give them a chance to prepare in advance. After all, they may be taking the heat from above and would appreciate a heads up.

Offer to pitch in when the team is in need (due to a low staff or absences). Offer to take work off of your manager's desk. Gain their trust and you will get the benefit of the doubt (especially if a complaint call rolls in from a customer). If they know you try your best and are a hard worker, they will defend you when others who may not know you as well try to throw you under the bus.

Learn your manager's personality and how to approach them when issues come up. Don't interrupt them during important meetings. Ask for their feedback and what you can work on to improve. Show initiative and if you want to move up to the next level have these discussions on how best to get there during your career meetings. Are their training opportunities available? Your manager will usually be supportive of these requests.

Sometimes, however, you will have a personality clash with your boss. Try to keep it professional and continue to work hard. It will eventually be noticed. That manager may not be in place for long if they are having the same issues with other team members. Perhaps working on a different team or in another line of business at the company could also be a possibility as a last resort. Sometimes there are assignment shifts in managers anyway, so you may not be in the same situation for too long.

However, despite the personality differences, a boss with a hard worker he/she can count on is going to typically support you in your endeavors and advancement.

AVOIDING CONFLICT

Unfortunately, you can't avoid a conflict on a claim file all of the time. But planning ahead and being timely will lead to less conflict down the line.

I like to prioritize and prepare a list of the top files that could either blow up at any time, have hostile parties involved that can quickly intensify, or the most significant exposures with management's eyes following them. If you take care of those items (and call people back timely) more often than not, you will be fine.

Inform your supervisor ahead of time if you have a case that may escalate or go to trial soon. If you want to set off a five-alarm fire, keep something like that quiet, and then watch how many people in upper management get involved!

You can usually figure out which customers will require a callback at lightspeed. They have left you a few messages within an hour and sound perturbed. Do not avoid calling them back; just get it over with. It always seems to escalate to another team member or manager if you ignore them and will just get you in hot water.

If there is a certain claimant you've already spent time talking to then make sure to thoroughly document the file. Some claimants may tell a story of you not calling them back but when they finally speak to your supervisor he/she can see how extensive your notes are and will see the extra time you've already spent with this customer.

MISCELLANEOUS TIPS

Don't shoot the messenger (claim assigner)

Now with paperless files it has mostly become a thing of the past. But if you still receive paper files on your desk, or have a person assigning you files, do not be known as the complainer. When I left a carrier, I was paid a nice compliment when told I would be missed because I was one of the few who did not give the assigner a hard time over files assigned.

Dress code (when in the office)

Make sure to look nice and presentable when in the office. Don't go overboard on those casual Fridays with ripped jeans and any type of inappropriate clothing. Dress for the position you want to have in the future. Especially if in a headquarters or corporate office location where higher-ups are walking by you.

Personal calls to a minimum

Don't get caught on the phone with personal calls often. Go for a walk on lunch and make your calls. Take a walk around the office. Avoid time-wasting and non-work conversations for long periods of time at your desk.

Microsoft Office for the assist

You may need an additional reminder for a high-priority diary. Set Microsoft Outlook reminders for important files. There are many other great futures you can learn about with regard to sorting incoming emails that are time savers. Post-it notes on your desk or screen may also still work in a pinch such as "Remember to adjust reserves upon receipt of new information," which is a classic adjuster reminder.

Tough tasks in the morning

Don't avoid making the tough calls. Tackle them head-on and get them over with. They become worse when you procrastinate.

Answer your calls

Pick up the phone if you can when a call comes in. This goes back to time management. If you pick up the call and speak to someone it saves a lot of time versus letting it go to voicemail, checking your voicemail and then calling someone back. Phone tag may continue, and you might not get them again for some time (more precious time wasted).

Let customers speak

Be an active listener, do not interrupt. Especially when taking statements, think about what questions you should expand on from the info you just received. Don't just read from a script. You may be overlooking a key detail they just told you.

Ask open-ended questions to solicit a better response (not just a simple yes and no). People have a tendency to talk more when given the opportunity. Sometimes if you are silent the other party may talk more and fill the silence to uncover even more investigative information.

Out to lunch

Getting fresh air and going out for lunch is beneficial. Take a break, go to the cafeteria or sit in your car. Talk with coworkers and get to know them. Be social. You need to recharge and stop staring at the computer screen from time to time.

Go for a walk. Some coworkers might bring sneakers and walk around the building on a nice day. Rest your eyes. Just don't sit at your desk. We have the habit of not wanting to leave our desk, but it is absolutely critical.

If you feel the need to continue to talk about work on lunch, then sit with colleagues and ask for advice on some of your current files. Just watch out for any food that may be hurled in your direction by colleagues who want to talk about anything else but work!

Pack a lunch (every now and then when in the office)

You will save a good amount of money, especially on gas from running out to eat every day. And you will get to know your coworkers better.

Positivity

Have a positive attitude. Others will take notice, especially of a bad attitude. Avoid that label.

The bare minimum is not enough

Don't just be a "steady Eddie." Look for opportunities to give suggestions and assist on special projects to help yourself stand out.

Breaks to refocus

Take breaks! If you are a desk adjuster get up and rest your eyes. Move around the office.

Trust is earned

Gain trust in your manager. Prepare ahead for meetings and with reports when it is your time to shine. Volunteer to assist and be a leader.

Career goals to the forefront

Continue to have career discussions and check-ins with your manager so you can get to the next level. Sometimes you just need a quick pep talk from your direct supervisor to feel good about your efforts.

Use your PTO

Take mental health days off! You need a break from time to time to recharge. Take them and enjoy. Prepare in advance for your time off so you can be stress-free.

PART 5: THE 9 KEYS TO CLAIMS VICTORY

1. BE A GOOD LISTENER

As an adjuster you will take many statements from insureds and claimants. But as I have said before, ask yourself if you are truly listening and comprehending the statements in which you are taking. An active ear can go a long way in uncovering that additional information that would otherwise escape someone who simply reads off a script of standard claims questions.

Whether it is the claims intake unit on the task or directly through the assigned adjuster, the first statement regarding a new loss is of the utmost importance. In some instances, it may be the only time you speak to the involved party. Quite possibly your one shot before a claimant is attorney-represented or an insured obtains a public adjuster. For that reason, it is imperative to extract all the information you possibly can early on while the claim is in its infancy.

This first interview is not just for simply "receiving language through the ears." Active listening takes this a step further and includes a higher level of effort.

Take your time, process the information and dig deeper. You'll notice a big difference in the quality of your statements and their effect on the case.

2. BE TIMELY

Arriving first usually ensures the best chance of success. True in life, and of even greater importance perhaps in the claims world.

The "early bird" adjuster is assigned a new notice of loss, where the information is brand new and readily available. In stark comparison is the claim reassignment. Being the second or third owner of a case puts you at a major disadvantage.

Missing statements with witnesses that are long gone, photos that have magically disappeared from the file and the insured's blurred view of prior events are just a few of the common struggles. The advice to "treat the file like your own" is immaterial because if it were indeed your own, you would have attempted to call the insured within the first two weeks to mitigate the flood of complaint calls.

Make the appropriate phone calls and follow-up attempts immediately. Each carrier has its own requirements, whether it's two hours or two days for contact. A recorded statement may take more effort upfront but is a transfer adjuster's dream, assisting in potential arbitration or litigation work.

Request the police or incident report. Use your phone call with the insured to obtain the case number or further details to make it a more accurate request with fewer delays.

Preserving the evidence right away is equally important. If the incident was recorded on CCTV, make sure the insured knows to preserve the tape. Our "DIY" society may encourage insureds to undertake their own repairs after a pipe break loss if an adjuster is not timely. Instead of trying to piece together what happened weeks after a repair through photos, a non-itemized plumber's invoice and some old parts; assign an engineer to arrive on the scene as soon as possible. The cost of the expert will save money in the long run, result in great customer service and a much happier subrogation team.

For a "notice only" liability claim we tend to subscribe to the theory that the best idea is to not contact anyone to avoid inviting a claim. Frequently, however, the decision has already been made whether to pursue one so wouldn't it be better from a customer service standpoint to reach out for a statement, show compassion and get an idea of an exposure now? A timely investigation avoids surprises, allows the setting of accurate reserves and likely leads to lower expenses in the end.

If you have too many claims, voicemails and emails to return, you need to prioritize them. Avoid investigative tardiness. Re-organize your day and move on the fly. Do you really need to completely work all your new claims today or can you focus on the initial contacts and get them out of the way?

Typically, one can predict when the wave of new losses will arrive and you can try to schedule your calendar ahead for a lighter day. It may also be a day that your teammates are out of office. If you are hit unexpectedly with new claims, re-prioritize your diaries and make sure to avoid distractions. Perhaps a teammate is willing to assist with an after-hours contact? Brainstorm with your manager for ideas on how to stay ahead of your contacts. Can you dig deeper into ISO searches for additional contact options?

Working a file early definitely pays off. Whether we need to comply with state laws, preserve the available evidence at the scene, or speak to our insureds while the events are still fresh in their minds, all claims benefit from a timely and thorough investigation upfront.

3. BE ACCURATE IN COMMUNICATIONS

As a society that is now communicating more through texting abbreviations and emoji's, there's an increase in errors through our written communications. These permanent blunders are costing companies real money and an uncalculated loss of credibility, especially when inaccurate emails or letters are sent to policyholders who may question the continued investment of their premium dollars.

Consider the claims letters that adjusters deliver to customers (or fail to) that could translate to real dollars lost. Perhaps a mitigation of damages or a rental car cutoff letter to a claimant has the wrong date or year. Maybe a bodily injury release lists incorrect parties, has misspelled or missing language, or how about a policy cancellation letter? Confusion may then increase the volume of phone calls to claim operators and the red voicemail button flickers with complaints at the supervisor's desk.

Today, many claims adjusters need assistance with basic business letter communications. The trend of copy and paste techniques may begin when an adjuster asks a colleague for help on a unique claim. A fellow adjuster may offer a "semi-related" letter (or e-mail) that will just need to be tweaked. Add in some laziness, time constraints and a quick press of the send button, and the letter gets into the hands of the policyholder prematurely. The "recycled" letter may have just a few small spelling or grammatical errors or may be completely off-topic. Insurance jargon is already confusing for customers without adding additional headaches.

Copy and paste or general errors on claim reports can be equally as damaging to one's career. Especially when it will be read by those who may not know the adjuster as well as an immediate supervisor. It is an opportunity to show the adjuster's worth and should not be taken lightly when writing a report or evaluation.

Society has changed. Handwriting and penmanship are almost a thing of the past. Cell phones and texting acronyms slowly butcher the English language. However, we need to embrace technology too, such as online apps and even the word-processing tools to help with spelling and grammar checks.

To improve sometimes we have to walk away. Writing a letter and staring at a computer screen is difficult without breaks. Taking a fresh look the next morning can help fine-tune a freshly created letter. Printing out a report and making handwritten edits is also an option. A coworker or supervisor can act as a second set of eyes.

When errors are captured in a formal written document, no one looks good; not the company, and definitely not the adjuster in terms of future career prospects. Always dedicate the appropriate amount of time for proofreading to guard against the copy and paste conundrum. Take ownership by showing that you care. If not, those permanent communications always have a way of coming back to haunt you.

4. BE PREPARED IN NEGOTIATIONS

It's time to settle the most onerous bodily injury case in your inventory. The medicals have been evaluated and you've scheduled a time this week to open the negotiations with the claimant attorney. This three-year-old file is ripe for resolution. The diary is set to flash on your screen. Are you ready for battle?

It is crucial to be prepared for the negotiation from the start. Know your file! The claimant attorney may have 10, 25, or 40+ clients and may not be an "expert" with the nuances of the case like you can be. Their negotiations may even dance around similar injuries of their other clients (neck and back being the most common). Read the medicals in detail. Ask for missing records if something does not add up. Check the doctor's release notes and enlist the assistance of a handwriting expert if needed (the best argument can often be what their own doctor documented hidden deep in the 200 pages of medicals that the attorney glanced over casually).

In all negotiations, be sure to make a list of your strengths and weaknesses. Understand the direction the attorney will go to argue his key points and be prepared for counterarguments.

(Yes, I understand that your client had quite a bit of pain and suffering, as you are stating, but on their release date, they reported a 1 of 10 pain scale, so your argument they are still in excruciating pain is difficult to fathom based on what you've provided).

Don't get into a dollars-based negotiation. Often attorneys may try to trick the adjuster into a back and forth of only numbers without regard to the details of the case. Let the facts lead in the negotiation and the dollars will follow along.

(Make me understand better why your client is deserving of another $10,000 increase in the offer, what am I missing in my evaluation based on the medicals you have provided me?)

Concessions and deviations (when supported by facts) are perfectly acceptable. Sometimes just a call before negotiating can also let the adjuster assess the style and technique of the other side. Your initial call with the attorney's demand may let you ask questions to see how they came up with their number. You are not forced to make a counter right away. That initial call may let you know that you need additional preparation before you are ready. You can also adjust your negotiating style if need be. Remember to be an active listener.

Always consider the intangibles. The injuries and treatment are one aspect but is their aggravated liability, potential credibility of witnesses on either side, permanency such as scarring (valued differently on everyone) or an impact on their daily lifestyle following the loss (unable to enjoy life's pleasures post-accident)?

Can your medical evaluation benefit from a claim nurse reviewing the file or an additional doctor's review to understand the case notes?

Patience is a huge factor in negotiations. It does not need to be finalized in one phone call!

Remain professional even if your adversary is not. That can be a barrier to settlement. Your opponent may not have a case they are confident about and can use a harsh tone to try to intimidate the adjuster.

A former manager offered me some unique words to live by when negotiating. He would explain to the attorney that at the end of the day, let's arrive at a number that is appropriate for the case. If it doesn't make either of us overly happy, that's fine, as long as we are both equally unhappy!

You will rarely find yourself performing cartwheels at the culmination of the claim. Still, with the right amount of preparation (and knowing your file), you can certainly position the settlement closer to your intended goal.

While this example of a negotiation involved a bodily injury claim, the lessons apply to all areas of adjusting. Information is your friend. Prepare appropriately so you can gain an advantage in negotiations.

5. BE CREATIVE

Sometimes to attain your goals, you need a little creativity in order to avoid a roadblock in claims. An example is handling bodily injury claims when you cannot obtain a pertinent update from the claimant attorney, and you sit with an inaccurate reserve on the file for months. You have no idea what sort of treatment is going on.

Perhaps it's now been almost a year and you have yet to receive an injury update on your represented claimant. Your bodily injury reserve currently sits at an inadequate $2,500.

When the independent auditing team digs deep into your file it appears as if you simply clicked "copy and paste" for the last 10 claim notes in a row. Is there no new information available? The problem is you've been running into that same adversary, the personal injury receptionist/gatekeeper – as the broken record file notes read:

"Called Attorney Smith, not available. Left message with receptionist for injury update, attorney will return call."

We can be pretty sure that the personal injury attorney here has not taken a sabbatical for half the year and is simply avoiding your calls.

Perhaps he actually has no update, but that in itself would clearly be an update. Maybe he has not checked in with his client or ordered any records. Maybe he can't even locate his client. But likely there's information to be gathered so that you can properly adjust your file and post an appropriate reserve. Creativity might be just what the doctor ordered.

So how does this conversation go when speaking with the gatekeeper who answers the personal injury attorney's phone when you ring?

"Hi, this is Joe Claims, and I need to speak with attorney Smith to obtain an injury update on his client?"

"Oh, is this in regard to settlement?" the receptionist says.

"No, just an update, please."

"Oh, sorry, he is in court, let me take down a message."

Diary your file for three weeks, rinse and repeat. Six to nine months later, and this game continues until you make an effort to break it. Or it ends with a lawsuit, and the surprise is that this soft-tissue case now involves multiple back surgeries, and you have a grossly inadequate reserve to explain to your supervisor.

So, let's look at some different opening lines with the injury gatekeeper that may assist in acquiring the information you need:

"Hello, this is Joe Claims. I was looking to speak with Attorney Smith regarding his client Mr. Miller."

"He's in court right now can I take a message," says the gatekeeper.

"Oh really, that's bad timing because I wanted to discuss the possible settlement of the case."

"Oh, wait I just heard him come in, hold please for Mr. Smith."

(In this scenario an amazing sequence of events has taken place where the attorney is teleported from the courtroom straight to the office to take your call! I know this to be true because it has happened so often!)

"Hey this is Joe Claims looking for an injury update, can I speak with the attorney, paralegal or clerk assigned to this case."

(Asking for someone else who may have knowledge of the file.)

"Hello, how are you? I was wondering if you could help me out, I've

been trying for some time to get an update and I am curious about your client. Can you check the file and let me know if he/she is still treating and if the medicals are ready for review?"

(Going straight to the gatekeeper for the possible update.)

"Hello there, I am calling about resolving a claim for your client. Can I speak to the attorney assigned?"

(You are floating the possibility of a resolution to see if the gatekeeper will take the bait and pass you through to the attorney. It's true though because you may be able to resolve now if you can obtain the injury specifics finally.)

"I am calling for an update and understand the attorney is not in, can you provide his cell phone number and email so I can reach out to him?"

(Other communication avenues to pursue the attorney for an update.)

"Hello, I am looking to obtain some updated injury information on your client, can I speak to the attorney please as I just needed to confirm the soft tissue injuries alleged in this matter."

(Sometimes when you make a statement and it may or may not be correct the other party may feel the need to correct you and spill the beans. This type of question may lead them to tell you there was a surgery or something more serious so they can convey it holds more value.)

"Hello, I'm sorry I've left messages now 10 times in the last 5 weeks, can someone there help me? There has to be someone with knowledge of this case if the attorney can't speak to me?"

(The plea for human decency can also be a good approach depending on the audience.)

But when all else fails, sometimes a certified letter (if not

currently in suit) can be very effective.

Dear Mr. Smith,

I have left several messages over the last six months with your receptionist on XYZ (list all dates of attempts). I have yet to receive the courtesy of a response from your firm with regard to an injury update regarding your client.

Please provide me with an update in the next 10 business days or I will deem your silence as an indication that you no longer wish to pursue a claim and I will review my file for closure.

Thank you,

Joe Claims

Creativity can go a long way in many facets of claim handling and obtaining injury updates is no different. Whether you try similar approaches or simply just calls at different times of day, your efforts will show that you are being proactive in your attempts.

If you try the same call over and over without success, you can be pretty sure that the same results will follow.

6. BE A DECISION MAKER

There's a hesitation in the claims industry about making a quick decision. And why wouldn't there be, given all of the information and evidence that might be out there? What if your decision is incorrect? There are consequences for actions that could follow you around, whether the decision affects customer or claimant service, or especially come performance review time.

But do we always have the ability to obtain every little piece of available information? In most cases, the answer is rarely. Sometimes there is a need to make the call to settle and move onto the next, or to stop the expense payment bleeding and work the other 119 files in your inventory. Time is money, after all.

However, often is the case where an adjuster does not feel comfortable deciding and overanalyzes a claim that is ripe for settlement. Some enjoy "decision shopping" and straining the time of coworkers. While it's prudent to ask a teammate for advice, it doesn't extend to every single team member (on multiple occasions) and all three supervisors on the floor!

That fine line between seeking the appropriate information and overanalyzing is what separates the top claims decision-makers from the pack. A manager's dream is the hardy adjuster who requires little watering and sprouts flowers on their own. The type of adjuster who struggles to make a decision and disregards the time of others can be a supervisor's burden. The "analysis paralysis" gets old, and soon becomes a trend where the manager is sought to make the decision for the adjuster.

Adjusters who struggle with decisions should also consider the source of the advice they are receiving. While outside defense attorneys may think they have a great chance to defend a case at trial, give thought to their motivations. Your phone calls and emails to them are productive to a point, but once you have the info you need, it makes little sense to keep asking them for their input if none of the facts have changed.

Consider the scenario in which a new lawsuit arrives for an errors and omissions claim. A broker's documentation blunder resulted in a coverage gap between a primary and umbrella policy for the high net worth insured who is now potentially on the hook to fill the gap based on the claimant's damages. Is it always the best decision to acknowledge the new suit and send it off to counsel for a full review, filing of an answer, and to start the discovery process? Or could it be beneficial to request a 60-day extension to answer, determine the information surrounding the oversight, and begin to evaluate the case? What about calling the plaintiff's attorney and engaging in a quick negotiation to see if settlement is an option before incurring defense bills? Would that also save face with the insured's client if you were proactive and looked to extinguish the exposure as quickly as possible? Think about the fact that if liability is an issue now, it is likely to be the same in the future, so why not move towards a resolution? Obviously, there are appropriate cases to defend, but sometimes when we struggle on a decision, we can soon find ourselves at the steps of the courthouse in a mad scramble to resolve for an inflated price.

It is true that many of the top experienced liability claims adjusters have their battle stories, the tough decisions made where some resulted in "scars," taking a chance at trial when they could have settled. But they can stand behind the fact that they made the decision and were proactive instead of waiting too long and then dealing with a decision thrust upon them.

Ask any senior claims representatives or management if they have made a mistake on a case. They all have, but while they retain those scars, the valuable part is that they made the decision and it was a valuable learning experience in retrospect.

So, can you spot the claims decision-maker in a new-hire interview? The standard questions that are used could be "Tell me about a time you were faced with making a tough decision under a deadline with limited information. What happened? Did you have all the information you needed? Would you do anything differently in hindsight?"

Can you always get an answer from the candidate? Maybe not, maybe they dance around the question, which is a good indication where they may fall. Perhaps a senior claims representative could fit into the interview process for a different perspective? Do they see this candidate being able to make the big decisions they frequently make with the proper training and practice? Would a simple take-home test or follow-up questions of a hypothetical scenario be a good idea? When (or perhaps, if) a candidate sends the thank-you email for the interview, how about a response to them with a real-life adjuster question to assess critical thinking?

Also, think about your direct reports. How do you change their thinking and confidence? How do you develop decision-makers as a manager? Don't give them the answers; have them make the call before you provide your opinion. Perhaps being mentored by a senior adjuster can encourage such thinking. Let them know there are no wrong answers; they just need to back up their stances with sound reasoning. Do you encourage "decision shopping," or is it recognized as a habit to use only sparingly? Can you use an example of "decision shopping" as the basis of a unit training session? In fact, it is clearly recognized that regular training sessions are a means to help staff develop strong decision-making skills that are founded in confident knowledge.

At the forefront, we are not talking about making a claims decision in haste or ignoring key information. We want to develop the critical thinkers to make decisions and learn a valuable lesson they can use in the future. That is how we grow as adjusters.

Gather your information, consider the avenues to get to your decision and potential consequences, make the call, and move on. The claims will keep coming and you'll never be without a new one. There will always be another file in need of the next big decision.

7. BE ETHICAL

A claims adjuster settles an auto liability claim with an unrepresented claimant for an unbelievably low amount, and the crowd goes wild! He is the envy of his fellow claims professionals and high-fives are spread around the office. How on earth did he get the claimant to accept such a number? The claims professional is on cloud nine—until his supervisor sits him down to discuss the situation further.

Doubt enters his mind as he hears, "Wow, that was a really low number to settle this case. Did we pay what we owe?"

The phrase "All that glitters is not gold," popularized by Shakespeare, speaks to this type of settlement that claims professionals undertake directly with a claimant—a situation that just doesn't feel right inside. How do we balance paying the lowest number possible with making the claimant whole and paying a settlement that is fair for both sides? Taking advantage of a claimant's lack of knowledge, unfamiliarity with negotiations and need for money is not ethical in the adjusting world, and while this isn't an overly common occurrence, it is something we need to be mindful of as claims professionals.

Some claims personnel would say that they prefer an attorney-represented claimant over dealing with one who is not represented. It's true that a lot of time is spent on explanations, education about the process, building trust, and knowing that it may all be for naught—months of time and effort can go down the drain as an attorney promptly ends your previous negotiations and is less motivated to work quickly on his new case. However, there are steps that liability claim professionals can take with claimants to avoid this scenario and work toward an amicable settlement for both sides.

First, it is important to be prompt and courteous from the start.

Establish timely contact and explain the process clearly and with set expectations. Empathy goes a long way and letting the claimant know the lines of communication will always be open builds trust.

Next, consider the situation from the claimant's perspective. Each morning, they walk out to the car and see the damage; it's a constant reminder of the loss and the accompanying frustration. The anger may be directed at the insurance carrier when calls are not returned immediately or at all. Placing yourself in the claimants' shoes will help you understand where they are coming from, and you can show them you are there to try and put this event behind them. A personal rapport will go a long way when you are asking for cooperation (for example, when you request a medical authorization to order records or to move the car from a storage facility).

To get a better handle on your claimant's status, check-in continually and don't let too much time pass while she is actively treating. If you're going to take longer to reach out to her, let her know when she can expect a call. Always start by asking how she feels and show empathy, which will more likely lead to a substantive update from the claimant.

When the situation calls for it (and claimants have revealed that their treatment has ended or is limited), you can consider a settlement in light of the expenses. However, if they indicate that they are still in pain or have questions about treatment, it is best to reiterate that they should fully seek any medical care they need because once a release and a check are issued, the process is over.

To achieve success, claims professionals should focus on the "three T's": **trust, transparency, and time**.

The **trust** factor is crucial when dealing with an unrepresented claimant. Did you call her back when you said you would? Did you provide appropriate customer service and order her records in a timely manner? Have you updated her throughout the claims process, and have you delivered on promises?

The next "T" is **transparency**. Have you articulated everything she needs to know? Are you hiding any key details? Did you withhold the fact that she is welcome to seek medical attention, or that she has the option to get a rental car while hers is in the shop? Are you fully explaining how you came up with your settlement offer and why it applies to this case, given the specifics?

Make sure to use words that are generally understood. Reporting that the claimant's MRI notes degeneration and disc desiccation may not be fully comprehended. Perhaps this is a pre-existing condition that was made worse by the accident. There is still pain and suffering, inconvenience, and the time it will take to get back to how she was feeling prior to the accident to discuss.

Be transparent on how you package your settlement offer and encourage the claimant to ask questions. Her first instinct may be that the insurance carrier is trying to pull a fast one, so show that you are an open book and your evaluation is well thought out with numerous considerations. Remember to actively listen to her concerns.

Finally, the release closes out the claim, so be sure that the claimant knows that once the release is executed, she gives up consideration to pursue anything further against the carrier or insured.

The last "T" is **time**. There is a lot of time involved in a claim, and you must treat the claimant with kid gloves. Perform to the best of your abilities, and you can settle the claim for a fair amount for both sides. If the claimant runs to an attorney, then you may not necessarily pay more to settle the case, but the process will drag out. Ultimately, that leads to more expense dollars and a file that you will likely be working on for two years with an attorney when you could have possibly settled quickly with the claimant.

The following are some claimant statements that you may run

into, along with tips on how to respond:

"The settlement number is too low; I know I can get more if I have an attorney."

The worst response would be telling her, "Get a lawyer and risk losing a third of your settlement." That response is confrontational and insinuates that the claimant is inept and does not understand she will lose money if she obtains an attorney. It can turn into a direct challenge for her to go out and get one just to prove you wrong.

The truth is that, in some venues, the attorney may be able to get more, but usually the injury value remains the same and the additional expenses will cost the insurance carrier moving forward. Defense costs, experts, surveillance, and medical record reviews will rack up costs, and those are real dollars to the carrier.

A less confrontational approach would be to advise that your offer was based on an evaluation of the medical records with many factors considered that you can explain further. Let her know that she can consult with an attorney if she wishes regarding the value, but that if she does obtain one, you would no longer be able to communicate with her directly.

Additionally, you can gently remind her that most attorneys will take a percentage of the settlement and often the process takes longer to resolve. However, note that it is her absolute right and that she should take time to think about how she wants to proceed. If she wants to consider the offer and then set a date to speak again about her concerns, that is an option that can provide clarity.

"You said that your offer took into consideration the amount of treatment I had. I think I may need more treatment, so can we discuss a new offer?"

The claimant is hearing that you are only basing your offer on the number of visits she had. Advise her that there are many factors involved, but if she feels the need for more treatment, then that is what she should do to feel better because that is the number one concern. Show empathy that the injury and healing is at the forefront and the settlement is secondary. Advise her that you can diary the file for a few months and then she can check back in once she has received the treatment she needs to feel better. Set a time when you can speak again in the next few months.

Typically, a claimant who is just out for more money will end that right away and say she does not need more treatment but would like a higher number to settle. Again, it is paramount to show that you are not trying to rush her through a settlement. She may just want you to understand that she had more pain and suffering than she believes you are giving her credit for.

"I had to take a day off from work to go pick up the police report [or an associated inconvenience] and I want to be reimbursed for my time."

Whether you want to consider additional costs to lock down a settlement is dependent upon your standard work procedures at your company. The claimant can submit further documents to validate her new demand, and you can add onto your offer as you see fit as more facts come to light through discussions. Just remember that an open claim becomes more expensive each day that it drags on.

As claims professionals we all feel the need to settle a claim for the most competitive number possible. But we need to remember to always use honor and fair dealing with unrepresented claimants.

Ethical claims settlements come from experience in negotiations and values as well as open communication. If it doesn't feel right, then it probably isn't. Conversely, if it seems too good to be true, it probably is. If, as a claims professional, you feel something is off, then take a second look and remember not to waiver from your ethical responsibilities.

8. BE HIGHLY ORGANIZED

It is crucial as an adjuster that you stay highly organized. Those who are not will find themselves behind the eight ball, barely keeping afloat in a sea of incoming information.

For this topic, I'll refer to the work of long-time property claims manager Rod Patterson. He is the author of *Guard Your Gates: Simple Steps to High Productivity*.

Patterson discusses the information age that is upon us. It is easy to get overwhelmed as an adjuster through a barrage of incoming emails, documents, and phone calls so much that we may miss what is vital to our investigations.

The way to keep on track as professionals is to employ his method to "organize, defend and guard your gates."

One example is that many adjusters find themselves bogged down with phone calls coming from every direction. Literally, they may come from cell phones and their office or desk phones making them twice the time constraint. Why not forward your desk phone directly to your cell phone to simplify the process?

Another important topic is time management. Do not get into the unhealthy habit of procrastination. Also, remember to set diaries at the right time for appropriate follow-up. Check your voicemails, respond to emails timely and prioritize those that should be done so as soon as possible. Try to keep a high priority task list to make sure you are in control of your most complex cases.

Always be on the lookout for others who may try to "steal" your time. It's perfectly acceptable to say "no" if you do not have the time to talk to some people. You can always have a conversation at a later time when you have less important responsibilities to attend to.

Time management is of the utmost importance in claims so I encourage you to pick up a copy of Rod's book for more information pertaining to his system of helpful reminders. Organization is critical!

9. BE CUSTOMER SERVICE-ORIENTED

For the final key to claims victory, I'm turning to my colleague the "Insurance Elephant" who is known for his dedication to customer needs throughout the claims process. Patrick Kelahan's mantra is to "innovate from the customer backwards," which many entrepreneurs in the claims space fail to realize before it's too late. Take it away, Pat!

The insurance moment of truth has been and always will be the adjuster/claim customer interaction: prompt, empathetic, comprehensive, and fair.

So how do you become the best in customer service?

Be insecure.

You have got to figure someone is doing it better; that will drive you to always work to improve what you do.

Be the adjuster who responds promptly, every time.

Be the adjuster who sets expectations, then exceeds them.

Be the one who asks the customer, "What is it that you need to know/have done first?"

Be the one who thinks past that initial need and suggests other helpful services that the customer may not have thought of.

Be the adjuster who always has time to take the customer's call.

Have the position that no other customer is as important as the one with whom you are communicating right now.

Be the person who knows that some other person is being the aforementioned.

Again, be insecure.

Your customers will love the effort driven by that!

PART 6: THE ADJUSTER'S REFOCUS

ADJUSTER AFFIRMATIONS

Finally, I will leave you with some positive affirmations and quotes that you might find helpful when considering some of the challenges you may face as you navigate through the ups and downs of a career as a claim adjuster.

As adjusters, we interact with many people who have suffered significant losses. Whether that be damage to their home, their vehicle or even physically, they may range from the very minor to ones so large that they are life-altering.

Often, we become desensitized to that aspect since we work on so many different types of losses. To the insured, this may be the most important event going on in their life at the moment (or ever) and they need to deal with us to produce some sort of solution. There are many emotions involved, and we must realize that often we will be the subject of their projections and outbursts, but they are not meant to be personal attacks against us as individuals.

Adjusters may also be stressed for various other reasons than just negative phone calls or interactions. There may be extreme frustration with having too many diaries on our files that we cannot possibly handle. Or we may be slammed with an abundance of new claims. We might also be fresh off a heated argument with a public adjuster, attorney or claimant.

If you are feeling burnt out or bogged down with a laundry list of to-dos from your supervisor, or received a horrible trial verdict on a file, or whatever the case may be, it is essential to take a deep breath, relax and think about the bigger picture. Dial-up a coworker and vent. Sometimes you just need to talk about your problems in order to get them off their chest.

We all make mistakes, and our supervisors are more concerned with how we grow and learn from them than focusing on the past. Admitting our blunders, acknowledging them, and then planning how we are going to improve in the future is respected and shows growth as a professional.

If the following list does not specifically apply to your situation then create a few of your own. This will help you refocus and reprogram your mind, so you are able to combat your frustrations on the job and not sweat the small stuff.

At the end of the day, our everyday interactions adjusting claims do make a difference in the lives of many, helping them get back on their feet. We may not hear a thank you or receive a pat on the back very often, but we should not lose focus of how important our jobs are.

<u>Good luck on your Claims journey!</u>

1. This overwhelming feeling shall eventually pass.
(No one is ever caught up completely. More work, more job security.)

2. I choose to react positively to the situation I'm faced with.
(I will let go of what I can't change and do the best with what I can control.)

3. The situation is neither good nor bad, it simply is.
(I will not invest further emotions into this situation. I accept it for what it is.)

4. I help people and make a difference in their lives.
(Despite the negatives, I won't lose sight of the big picture.)

5. These obstacles are just learning opportunities.

(I possess successful qualities and will continue to develop them.)

6. Breathe in, breathe out and move on.

(Don't get caught up in one claim file or negative interaction. It should not take up all of your energy. Tomorrow is a new day for a fresh start.)

POSITIVE THINKING

"Spend eighty percent of your time focusing on the opportunities of tomorrow rather than the problems of yesterday."

-Brian Tracy

"Just one small positive thought in the morning can change your whole day."

-Dalai Lama

"You can't change how people treat you or what they say about you. All you can do is change how you react to it."

-Mahatma Gandhi

"The truth is that our finest moments are most likely to occur when we are feeling deeply uncomfortable, unhappy, or unfulfilled. For it is only in such moments, propelled by our discomfort, that we are likely to step out of our ruts and start searching for different ways or truer answers."

-M. Scott Peck

"Attitude is a choice. Happiness is a choice. Optimism is a choice. Kindness is a choice. Giving is a choice. Respect is a choice. Whatever choice you make makes you. Choose wisely."

-Roy T. Bennett

EPILOGUE BY THE INSURANCE ELEPHANT

(Patrick Kelahan)

HOW TO ACTUALLY BECOME A GOOD ADJUSTER

Unfortunately, for many insurance companies it's not as simple as "let's go to the talent store and pick up a few great adjusters."

But that's GREAT news for you, the prospective (or current) adjuster who is ready and willing to absorb every bit of knowledge thrown your way with unlimited opportunities ahead.

The truth is that effective adjusters are not trained in two weeks, two months, maybe even two years. There is no "owner's manual" to explain an adjuster's job, tasks, or rules. Not even this book, but it's a solid start!

Time and experience forge a good adjuster's skills, nuances, and abilities to serve well. NO ONE delivers a coverage denial well his/her first time that occasion is encountered. Or second, third, etc.

Companies value the relationships that senior staff develop with new hires; senior staff work to develop trainees because it's a self-preservation effort; if the new hire is trained well, the tenured adjuster doesn't get the additional pending claims. Fewer calls, fewer fires to put out, a modicum of control over one's work so to speak.

All this work invested in making a neophyte into someone who can assimilate all the roles of being an adjuster, all the details that a claim brings, and all within the environment of a claim organization.

The real goal? Develop the adjuster into someone who is empowered to make decisions, can condense all the details of a claim (and of course each claim is unique) into a format that leads the adjuster to a coverage or estimate or handling or settlement decision. To become a valued worker who is unafraid to decide what is best under the varied circumstances presented, what is best for the company and the customer.

Adjuster, defined - "An adjuster is charged with evaluating an insurance claim to determine the insurance company's liability under the terms of an owner's policy."

Well, that's one definition of an adjuster, but certainly an apt one.

A claim adjuster is someone who reviews, investigates, determines policy coverage for the claimed damage, composes/calculates an estimate of damage, and works with the insured to settle the claim based on policy coverage. Many moving parts to a claim, to a policy, to the regulatory and legal environment, to the customer experience. And generally, one adjuster to manage the customer and company requirements from first notice of loss to settlement.

Anyone who has not served the role of claim adjuster can read what the role is, observe the application of the role, give it a critical eye, speak of it, lament its shortcomings, etc., but it is a unique enough job that absent performing it the full understanding of the word "adjust" really being a key descriptor may not be fully grasped.

The claims customer knows what the presence of the adjuster is like but is unknowing of what makes an adjuster. No, the policyholder knows when the person with whom he is working acts like an adjuster because their claim moves forward in the adjuster's presence.

Like a clever magician, the outcome the adjuster provides is wondrous but the mechanism behind it does not matter to the audience. It's just a solution pulled from one's hat.

Insurance companies can succeed or fail based on adjuster abilities, performance, and service acumen.

Not individual by individual performance, but how the respective carrier organizes, trains, supervises, supports, trains some more, engages, and assesses its adjuster core; it is a competitive advantage.

A better way to summarize the role?

Adjusters are the "WD-40" of the insurance service world.

They can fix anything!

Chris Casaleggio

Chris Casaleggio, AIC, AINS, is an experienced casualty claims professional, having worked for several major insurance carriers. The author holds a master's degree in Communication from Arizona State University and has published numerous technical claim-handling articles in periodicals such as Claims Magazine, Insurance Thought Leadership, Property Casualty 360, Insurance Nerds, and CLM Magazine. In addition, his industry involvement has included co-writing the Burned Out Adjuster's Playbook: Learn How to Stop Stressing and Start Enjoying Your Job As an Insurance Adjuster. He also has contributed to the Successful Adjuster's Playbook: The Secret Skills for Providing the Best Claims Experience.

FEEDBACK

I greatly appreciate your financial investment in purchasing this book and your valuable time reading it. If you would like to leave a rating on Amazon or feedback, I would be extremely grateful.

Many thanks and best of luck on your Claims journey!

adjustingbook.com

Made in the USA
Middletown, DE
07 September 2023

38165268R00078